Basic Charting Techniques
Technical Analysis

Dana DeCecco

Former Commodity Trading Advisor

CFTC and NFA

Has published many books and articles about trading the markets

Copyright © 2014 Dana DeCecco

All rights reserved.

ISBN-13:978-1505380354

ISBN-10:1505380359

DEDICATION

Dedicated to the GOOD LORD who gave us all a brain.

CONTENTS

	Acknowledgments	i
1	Crazy World of TA	1
2	The Holy Grail	Pg #10
3	Trends	Pg #18
4	Fibonacci	Pg #23
5	Indicators	Pg #30
6	Candles	Pg #36

ACKNOWLEDGMENTS

FXCM Marketscope
Oanda FX
MT4 Metatrader
FreeStockCharts.com
Investopedia

1 THE CRAZY WORLD OF TECHNICAL ANALYSIS

The world of technical analysis has gone mad. The number of indicators available is mind boggling. We have indicators indicating if the other indicator has indicated! Novice traders have got to be confused.

Some of these indicators are very good at times.

Name		
Trend (7)		
	Os	AROON(Aroon) Reveals the beginning of a new trend.
	In	ARSI(Adaptive Relative Strength Index) Is a more flexible variant of Relative Strength Index.
	In	HA(Heikin-Ashi Chart) Helps to identify trends and trend changes more easily.
	In	ICH(Ichimoku) Enables to quickly discern and filter "at a glance" the low-probability trading set
	In	MD(McGinley Dynamic) McGinley Dynamic Indicator.
	In	REGRESSION(Regression Line) Is the linear regression line used to measure trends.
	In	SAR(Parabolic Time/Price System) Helps to define the direction of the prevailing trend and the moment to close po
Classic Oscillators (10)		
	Os	CCI(Commodity Channel Index) Measures the position of price in relation to its moving average.
	Os	CMO(Chande Momentum Oscillator) Measures overbought and oversold levels, trendiness and divergence based on
	Os	MACD(Moving Average Convergence/Divergence) A trend-following momentum indicator that shows the relationship between two
	Os	OSC(OSC Oscillator) Compares where a security price closed relative to its price range over a given

Actually ALL of these indicators are very good depending on MARKET CONDITIONS. The markets are constantly changing. The indicator that is working today may not be working tomorrow.

Of course we have many to choose from so we could use a different indicator each day of the month. This is really a bad idea. We need to know how an indicator behaves before we begin using it.

Basic Charting Techniques

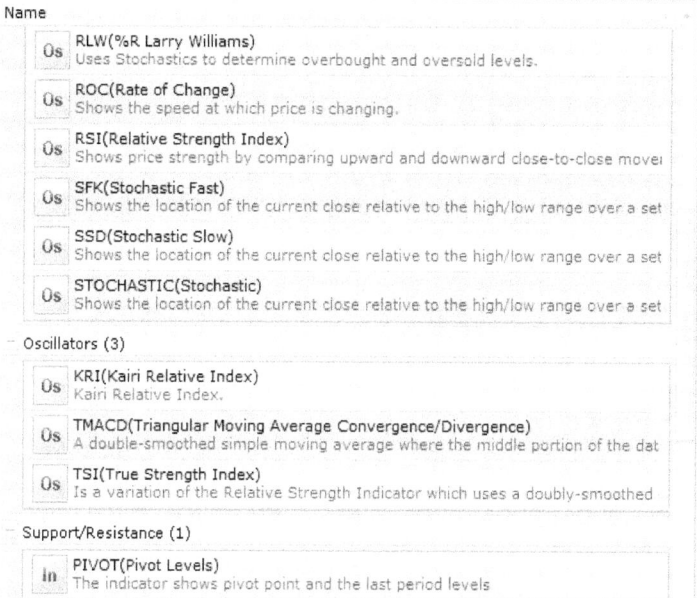

Do we really need all these indicators? Do professional traders use all these indicators?

The answer is NO. This is way to confusing for the human brain to figure out.

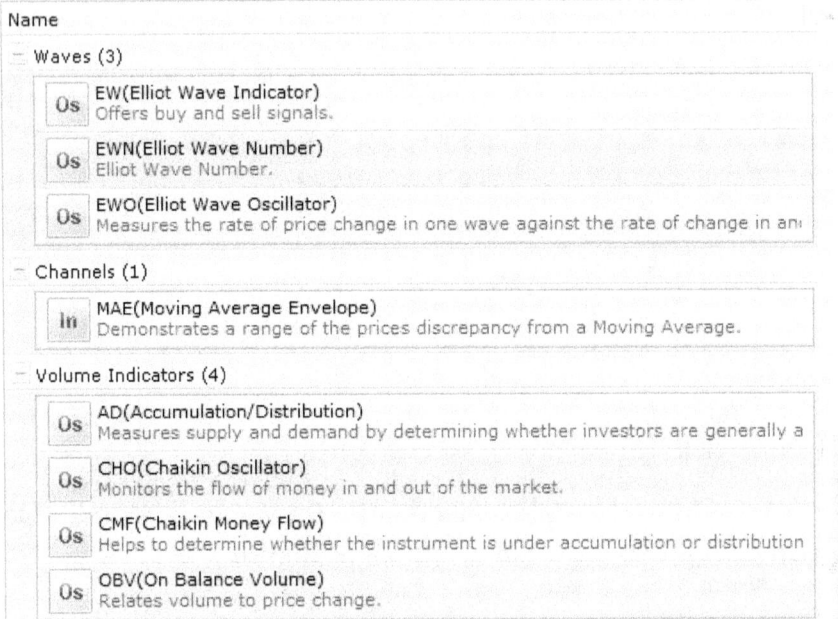

If you insist on using indicators pick out two or three and master them. Observe their behavior under various market conditions. Is the market trending or range bound? Is the market quiet or volatile?

In my early trading days I believe that I have tried all of these indicators and invented a few of my own. I still use two well known indicators, MACD and STOCHASTICS. I use them in a very limited way. Either for confirmation or divergence.

I would never develop a trading system with indicators. If it were only that simple. The "powers that be" know which indicators you are using. They have very deep pockets and can move the markets at will.

The average trader, or even the exceptional trader can not beat the institutional traders at their own game. They have all the chips and can bury us if they wish. The only option left for the average trader is to trade WITH the big boys.

Indicators provide us with a set of rules to trade by. Rules are absolutely necessary to all traders, big and small. The question is, what are the rules?

Most of the trading done today is program trading. The large trading syndicates, central banks, and institutional traders use computer programs to do the trading. It does not matter whether you are trading stocks, options, futures, or forex. Program trading is running the show.

A computer does not have a brain. Someone with a brain must instruct the computer. They must have a set of rules to trade by. The computer must be instructed of when to buy and when to sell any given asset.

The rules are programmed into the computer before the action begins. A fast computer can make many transactions per second. They could buy 1000 shares, sell 900 shares, buy 1000 shares, sell 800 shares, buy 1000 shares, and sell 700 shares in far less than a second.

That makes it very difficult for us to plainly see what is going on. They are very sneaky because they want all your chips. They are greedy and relentless. The market is a very scary place. Enter carefully and get out as soon as possible.

I don't mean to take the fun out of it. After all, you are trading with money you can afford to lose. Right? Even so, losing money sucks. Unfortunately, losing money is part of the trading game.

No matter how good your trading system is, you will suffer your share of losses. The idea is to have more wins than losses or bigger wins than losses. How about a few examples?

If we flip a coin one hundred times and each time you win you get two dollars and each time you lose it costs you one dollar, do you have a good trading system? Yes you do. The odds are in your favor because the payoff is higher than the loss on a 50/50 probability.

Trading is all about probability and odds, just like Las Vegas. We are taking a calculated risk each time we make a trade. The idea is to get the odds in your favor on each and EVERY TRADE.

If you created a trading system that lost two out of three trades and the wins paid five dollars but the losses cost two dollars, this would be a good trading system. At the end of the day you would be net profitable.

If you created a trading system that won nine out of ten trades, the wins paid one dollar and your one loss cost ten dollars, you would have a losing system. You get the idea. It's all about odds, probabilities, cost, and payoffs. You will always have wins and losses so get used to it. Losing is part of the game (but it still sucks).

Getting back to indicators, I do not believe the big traders use any indicators. In fact, I believe that they are partially responsible for the idiotic number of indicators that are available to traders. They want all your chips.

The more confused you are the more likely you are to make mistakes. But you can always blame the stupid indicator. I will give you odds that they are counting on it. But they still need to program something into the computer.

It's not the news because they do not know the news in the future. Or do they? Maybe they leak their version of the news to wire services and TV bimbos on CNBC. The fact is that they most definitely do.

Are you telling me that the whole show is fixed? Yes I am but there are other considerations. All of the "powers that be" are not on the same page. Computer wars rage frequently creating wild volatility swings.

Spreads are increased that create very expensive conditions to trade in. Under these circumstances there is no indicator that could be effective. The market makes no sense. Unless you know what is going on.

Most market conditions can be effectively traded if you understand the forces that are moving the market. CNBC will tell you that the "investors" blah...blah...blah. This is total nonsense. I have seen markets move 300 points in a minute or two. Surely, all those investors could not possibly be online at the same time. Yet, people believe all this BS.

Of course, the "powers that be" cannot confiscate all the money from investors because the game would be over. They need to let the buy and hold investors make some money. And they do. If the markets don't remain somewhat stable it's game over for everybody.

Price fluctuations in a stable market have to be there. They are commonly referred to as market corrections. Traders call then Fibonacci retracements. This is where the money is made for traders.

Market participants are not necessarily in the market to make money trading. The commodities market is a prime example. A farmer selling corn may enter a futures contract just to secure a profit on his crop of corn. He doesn't care what the traders do because he has secured the price for his corn crop.

Kellogs may enter a futures contract to buy the farmers corn to make corn flakes. The price they will pay for the corn is locked in and they do not care what the traders do.

A foreign auto maker may have sold a contract to deliver 10,000 cars. If they will be paid in US Dollars they may want to buy a put contract on US Dollar futures as insurance. If the value of the Dollar declines they will still recover the initial sale amount.

So you see, everyone is not in the game as a trader. Traders are in the game specifically to make money on market fluctuations. It is a dangerous game for a small trader and he better have his act together before jumping in.

This brief publication should get your act together enough to get your feet wet. I try to keep my books brief and to the point but don't overlook the nuggets of wisdom. Everything I write is important. I'm not trying to fill up space on the page.

The points that I will cover are basic trading methods. That is all I ever use, just the basics. At least to me they are the basics. I have been trading for so long, I often forget how much I know. I have probably been where you are going.

Technical analysis is the subject of this book. Although fundamental analysis is very important, I believe it has already been priced into the chart. The big traders are light years ahead of us. Economic news releases are simply an excuse to manipulate the price.

I avoid trading during economic announcements.

2 THE HOLY GRAIL

If there is such a thing as "The Holy Grail" of trading it has got to be SUPPORT and RESISTANCE. There is absolutely, positively nothing more important in the arena of technical analysis.

Support and resistance areas occur in all time frames. The higher the time frame, the more weight the S/R line carries. Consider the following forex example.

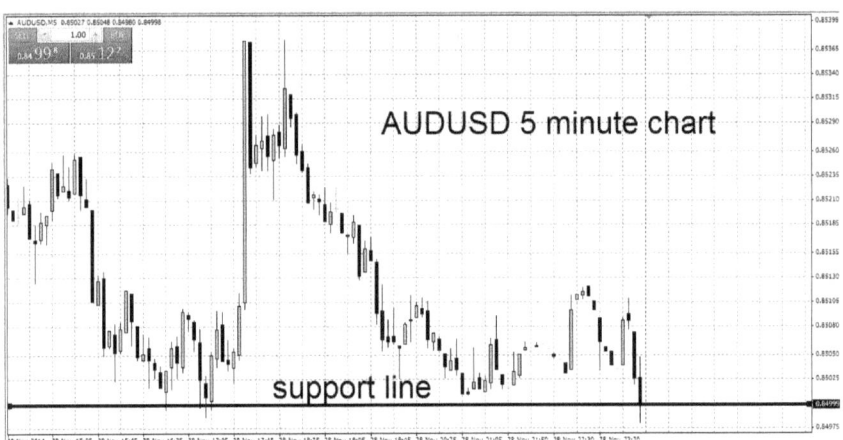

This is a 5 minute chart of AUDUSD. The price is sitting on support verified by the previous 2 failed attempts to break through support. We would not base any trade just from the information available from a 5 minute chart.

We will get a better idea of what is going on if we view the big picture.

Basic Charting Techniques

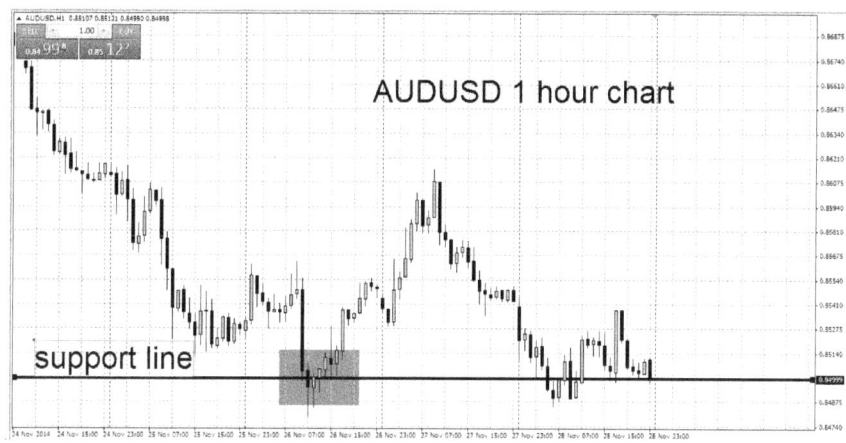

Here is the AUDUSD 1 hour chart. Each candlestick equals one hour. The shaded gray area shows a previous attempt to break through the area of support. Lets see if there is any activity on this line at a higher time frame.

This particular support line has gone back for years making it a very important and powerful area of support.

This is a pretty good trade setup for a long position. The best trade setups occur when the price is very close or dead on a S/R line.

Here is a stock example of SIRI daily chart.

We will jump to the weekly chart to see if this resistance line has significant value.

Jumping to the higher time frame will evaluate our S/R line. It will help us to determine the strength of the support or resistance. There is a better way to do this.

Jump to the daily chart and scroll back in time. This is a very accurate method to determine S/R strength. The following example is the forex pair GBPUSD, the British Pound and the US Dollar.

Jump to the daily chart, one candle equals one day.

Now we scroll back through time.

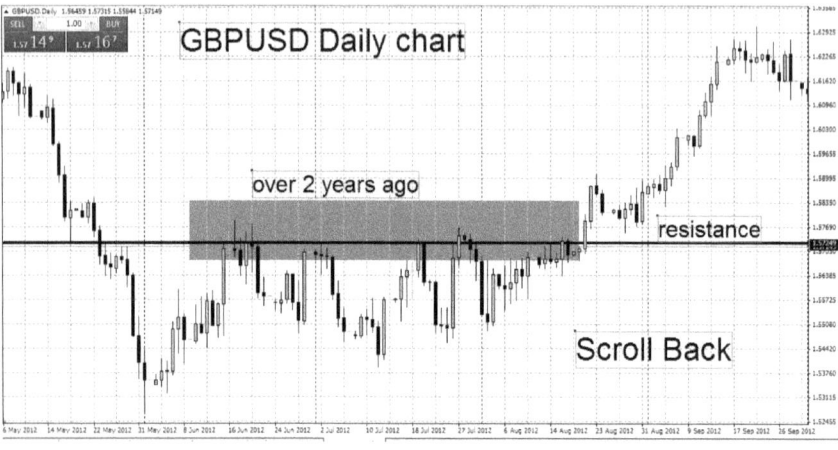

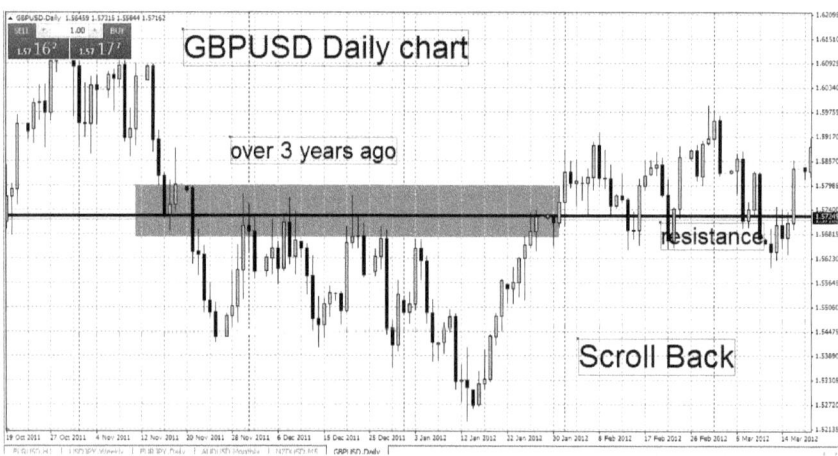

If we continue scrolling back the results could be surprising. I have scrolled back over 20 years on some of these S/R lines.

I don't know why these specific areas are important but they are important to someone. My guess would be Central Banks in the case of forex.

As price approaches these areas look for candlesticks with long wicks and long tails.

It is up to you to determine the strength of the S/R line. With a little experience it should be easy. The entire process takes less than a minute. I have produced videos on this subject. Go to YOUTUBE and enter my name – Dana DeCecco.

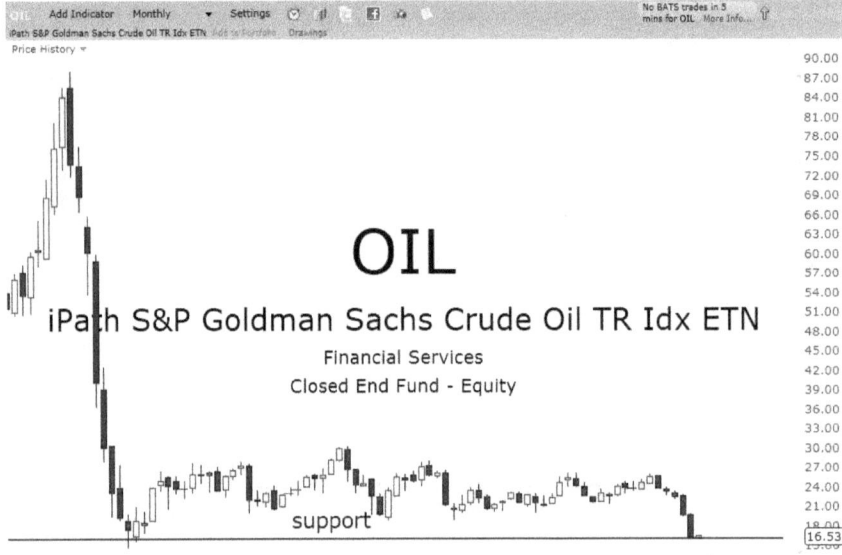

This is a monthly chart of OIL. It is sitting on VERY STRONG SUPPORT.

Basic Charting Techniques

This is a weekly chart of GOLD. It is up against weak resistance.

Checking the S/R lines is fast and easy. It is also the most important step you can take before entering a trade.

If the price is not on a S/R area then it is TRENDING up or down. The trend is your friend until the end. The end of the trend is when price runs into support or resistance. The price may sometimes stall at the S/R and the trend may continue.

2 TREND LINES

After viewing a million or so charts I can easily determine if an asset is trending or consolidating. Drawing trend lines only takes a few seconds and it is a good visual aid.

The forex pair EURUSD followed a distinct trend line down for eight months.

The hourly chart displays the counter trend during the major downtrend. The length of your proposed trade will determine the time frame you are using.

Viewing the three charts above I would be inclined to enter a short trade on EURUSD. I am basically a short term trader and do not enter trades lasting for months. Most of my trades last from a few minutes to a few days.

Notice the double top at resistance. Double tops are one of my favorite divergence strategies. I will discuss divergence in another chapter. It is one of the few trades that I actually use an indicator.

When drawing your trend lines, draw the line on the bottom for up trends and on the top for down trends. The correct entry is a bounce off the trend line in the direction of the trend. For a down trend enter a short position. For an up trend enter a long position.

Moving averages are a common indicator widely in use. As with any indicator, they are either being used on a particular asset or not. Look at the chart. If price has been bouncing off the moving average it is likely to continue. I use the 50 and 200 day simple moving average.

On both of the above examples I would normally enter a long position. Place your stop loss just below the MA line but not too close. They will usually bump the price down briefly to take out your stop loss.

If the daily price CLOSES below the MA this would be confirmation for a short position. We would only use this indicator in conjunction with our support and resistance lines. We must use all the tools in our arsenal.

I use LINEAR REGRESSION channels quite often. The formula is complex but it is more or less the average of prices.

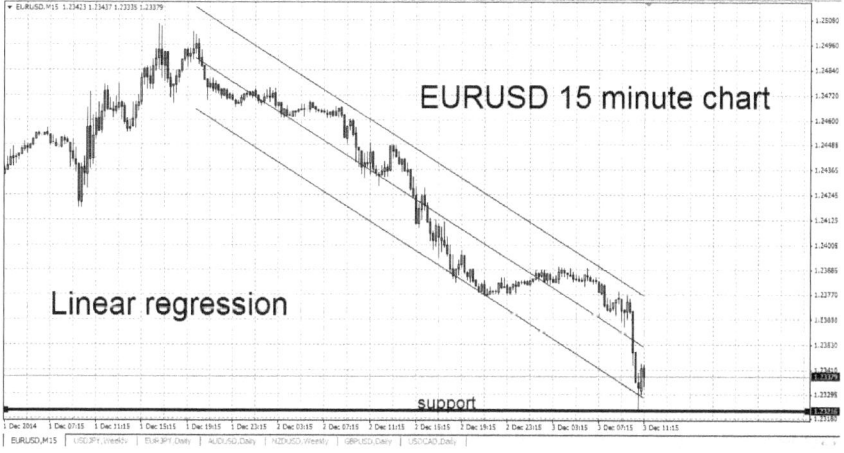

The price in this chart has bounced off the lower regression line which also corresponds with major support. These two signals would indicate a long position. Do your homework before entering any trade. These actions will become second nature after a while and they only take a few minutes.

Here is a long trade set up on the forex pair GBPUSD. Notice The shaded box. They briefly dropped the price to take out stop losses. If you set your stop loss too close you will have more losses and if you set it too far away you will have larger losses but that is the game.

The following stock chart is provided for a very good reason. If there is no trade DO NOT TRADE. If you look hard enough you will invent a reason to trade. The best trades will be obvious.

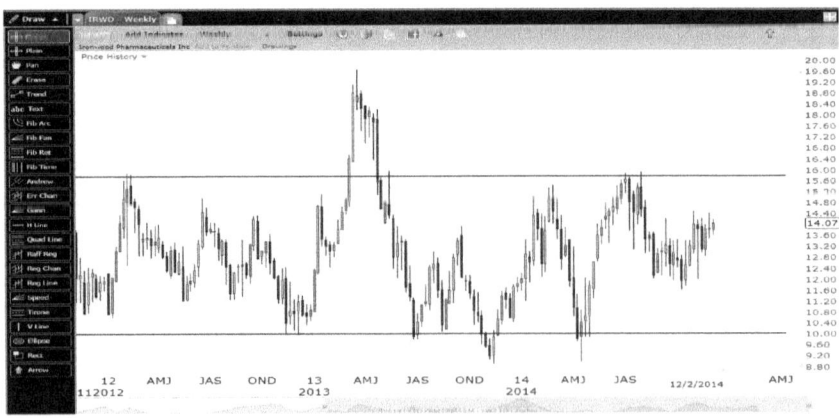

FIBONACCI

Fibonacci was a mathematician from the middle ages. You can read all about Leonardo Fibonacci on the web. The bottom line is that he discovered a sequence of numbers found throughout the natural world. These ratios have been applied successfully to modern day trading charts. Every available charting program offers Fibonacci tools.

The markets tend to respect these ratios for reasons unknown. We don't care about WHY it works. We do care about IF it works. Traders must realize if we find something that is working we use it. You do not need to analyze the WHY.

The following definition was borrowed from INVESTOPEDIA. I couldn't have said it better myself.

DEFINITION OF 'FIBONACCI RETRACEMENT'

A term used in technical analysis that refers to areas of support (price stops going lower) or resistance (price stops going higher). The Fibonacci retracement is the potential retracement of a financial asset's original move in price. Fibonacci retracements use horizontal lines to indicate areas of support or resistance at the key Fibonacci levels before it continues in the original direction. These levels are created by drawing a trendline between two extreme points and then dividing the vertical distance by the key Fibonacci ratios of 23.6%, 38.2%, 50%, 61.8% and 100%.

Fibonacci retracements occur ALL THE TIME in ALL THE TIME FRAMES. WE know for certain that it will occur. We just don't know when.

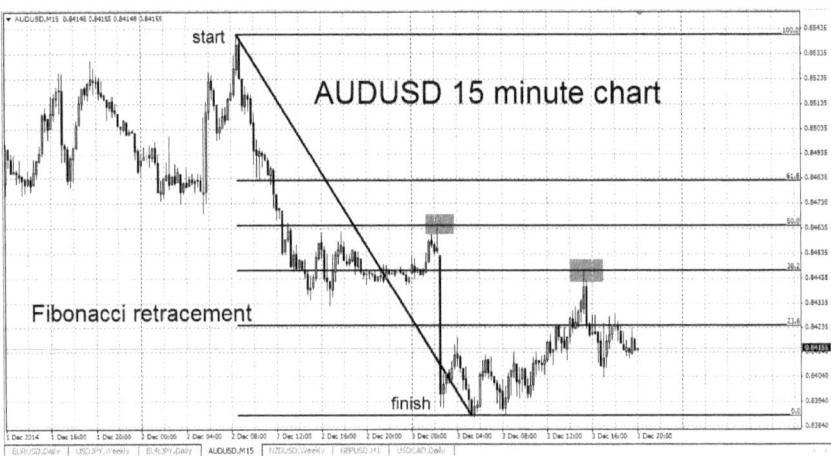

Notice how quickly and precisely the price touches these levels in the shaded boxes.

On the stock chart above notice how price closed on the Fib level but the high of the bar briefly surpassed the Fib line. This was done to take out the stop loss orders. Be careful with your stops.

Fibonacci retracements can be used for trading all assets including stocks, currencies, and commodities. Use this tool in conjunction with the support and resistance lines.

In 1935 H.M. Gartley published a book entitled "Profits in the Stock Market". Since then the pattern has been refined with additional parameters added, specifically Fibonacci retracement ratios. Gartley patterns are visible and measurable patterns that occur on technical analysis charts of various markets. These patterns apply to the Stock Market, the Commodities Market, and the Currency Market.

The Fibonacci based patterns can create bullish and bearish trading signals. The patterns must meet specific conditions to be considered a verified pattern. Key Fibonacci ratios are used to observe patterns that resemble and are similar to deformed "W" or "M" patterns within the chart. These patterns can be viewed on a few websites that can be found with a simple search. Other patterns have been developed that are similar to the Gartley pattern. They have been given names such as The Crab, The Bat, and The Butterfly.

The patterns consist of four distinct price points or pivot points on a price chart. They are considered classic retracement patterns and occur in all time frames. This makes these patterns usable for day traders, swing traders, and longer term investors. Gartley originally used ratios of one third and two thirds. It was not until further development of the pattern that the Fibonacci ratios were applied.

Gartley wrote that the pattern was successful approximately 70% of the time. Recent studies have reinforced this estimate. The pattern has been tested over the past 70 years making it a very reliable trading signal.

Larry Pesavento, a veteran trader of over 40 years, has done extensive research on this pattern. He published a book in 997 called "Fibonacci Patterns with Pattern Recognition".

When the pattern is properly identified, the trader can enter a high probability trade. The main advantage of this trade is the ability to set tight stop loss orders in case of pattern failure. As with any trading system, this pattern is best used in conjunction with other reinforcing indicators. Support, resistance, and pivot points would be an example of this.

This style of trading is sometimes referred to as Harmonic Trading. No trading systems work all of the time. A 70% win rate with a controlled risk makes this pattern based system an excellent trading system for many types of traders.

This is a universal trading indicator and can be applied to any market. Stocks, Forex and futures are examples of these markets. Since this indicator is published and available to the MT-4 Forex trading platform we will provide forex examples throughout this publication.

This indicator is called the ZUP Indicator (Zig Zag universal with Pesavento Patterns). I wrote other books on this subject because it is one of the most accurate indicators I have ever used. It can be downloaded to an MT 4 charting platform.

I will provide a few examples here. For detailed information refer to my book **"How to Trade The ZUP Indicator".** There is also information available on the web and in various trading forums.

The algorithm automatically generates buy and sell signals on the MT 4 platform. It should always be used in conjunction with S/R lines for maximum potential.

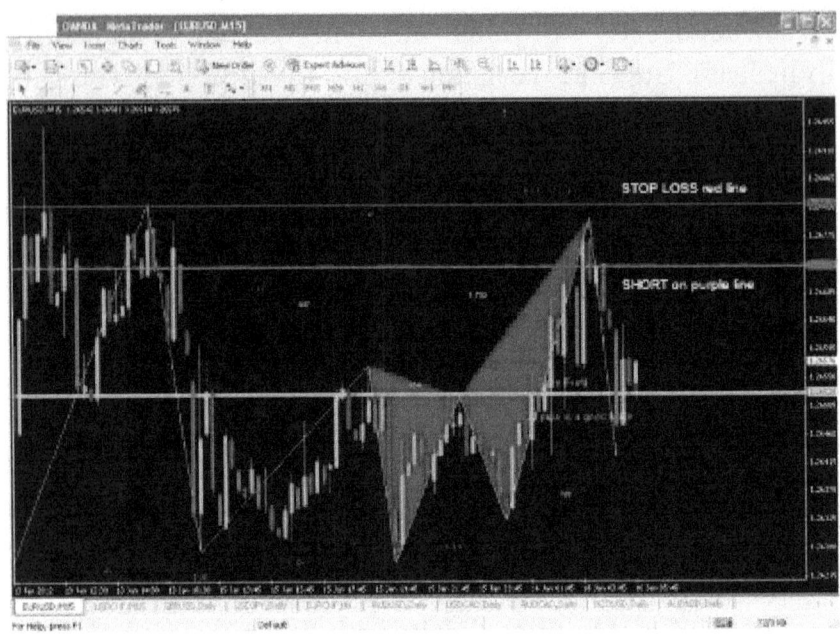

The horizontal lines represent the levels at which I placed my ENTRY, EXIT, and STOP LOSS orders.

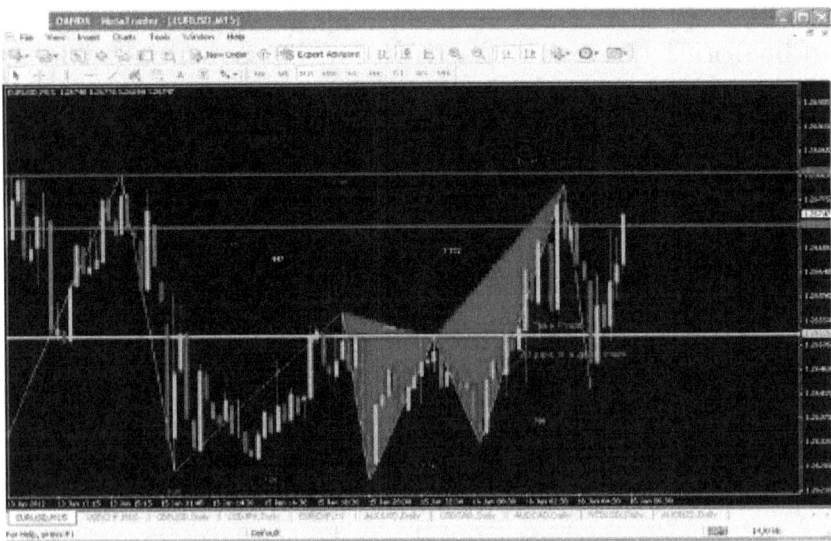

Basic Charting Techniques

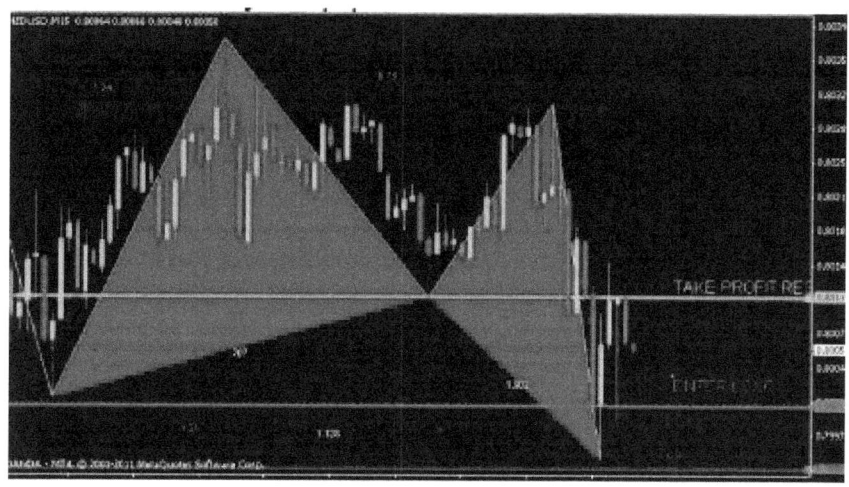

Signals can be generated in all time frames to suit your trading style, day trading to long term investing. If traded properly there is no better trading signal or system available.

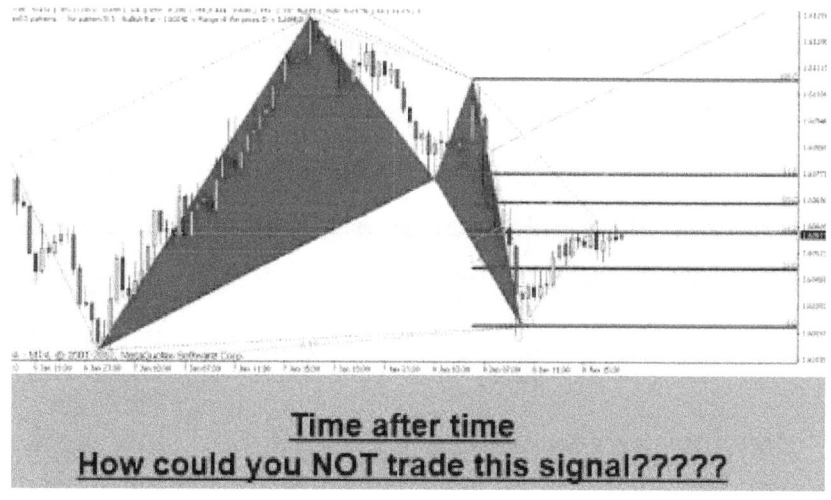

INDICATORS

I use indicators for two reasons:
CONFIRMATION and
DIVERGENCE

The STOCHASTICS and MACD indicators have been around a long time. These are the only indicators that I use and I use the preset settings.

I use stochastics for confirmation when trading consolidating markets. Those are chart patterns trading in a range or going sideways. They are not trending up or down.

I do not use stochastics as a trigger or trade signal. Once I have set up my trade using the signals provided in previous chapters I will check the stochastics to see if they conform to the price chart.

Ranging markets generally occur during slow market hours. During times of less volatility or trading activity the price tends to oscillate in a channel.

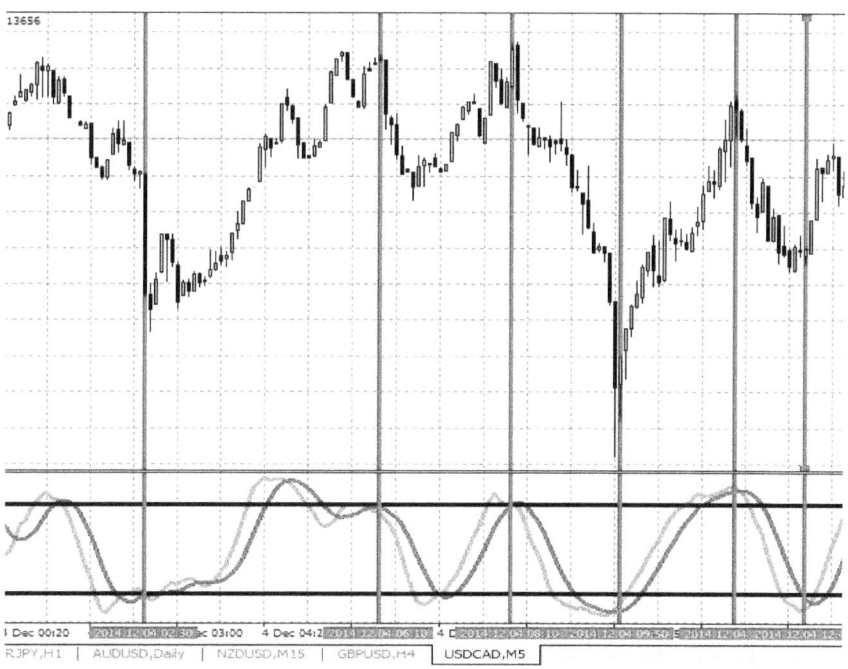

The stochastic indicator will usually confirm the predictable price action.

One of the oldest and most dependable trading systems that I use is DIVERGENCE. This is the only indicator based system that I use. This system works well with the double top, double bottom and the "head and shoulders" chart patterns. I use the MACD indicator and have occasionally used stochastics.

Divergence means that the price is going one way and the indicator is going the other way. The indicator is usually correct and price will change direction. This system should not be traded during high volatility times such as economic news releases.

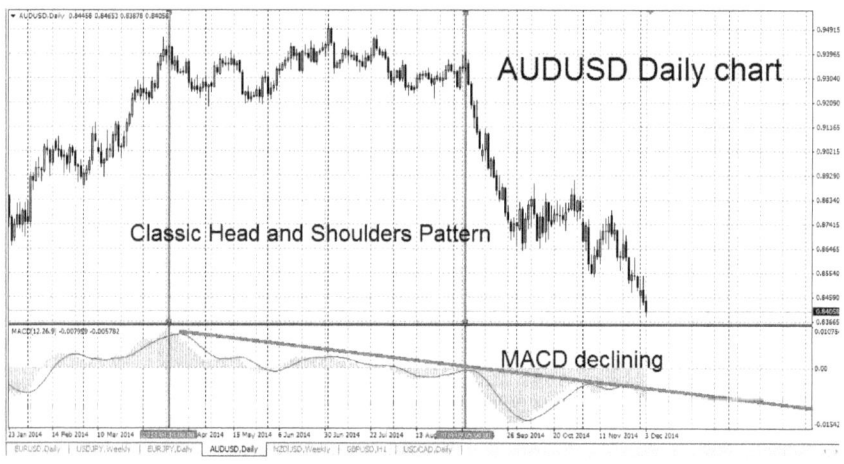

Throughout this head and shoulders pattern the MACD continued the decline giving us a highly predictable trade setup. This divergence system works in all time frames. I generally use the 15 minute charts while searching for double tops and bottoms which are very common.

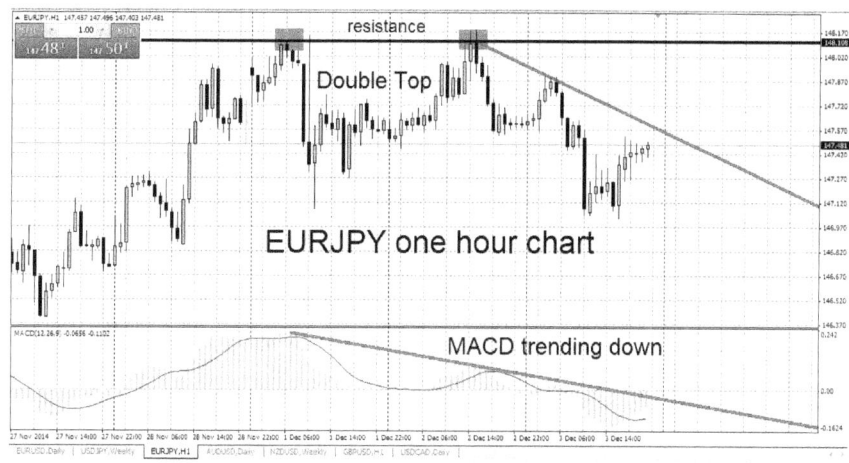

This trading system works equally well for stocks, commodities, and currencies. The correct entry is the bounce off the resistance line in the above chart.

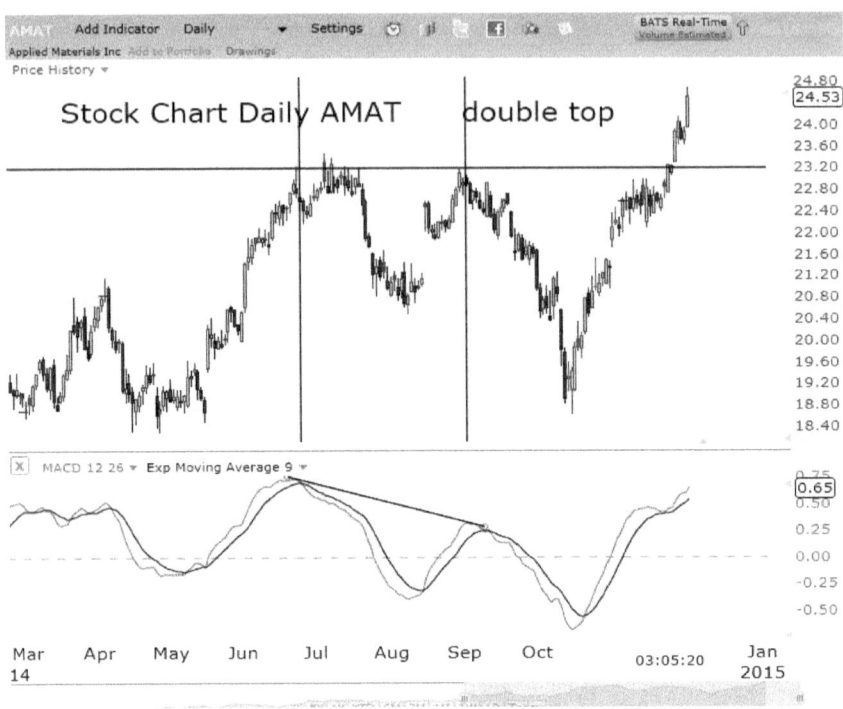

This is the easiest system to learn and trade. Just insert the MACD indicator on to the charting platform and start flipping through assets. You will find a number of double tops and bottoms. If the chart pattern corresponds with a major S/R line you will have a very high probability trade.

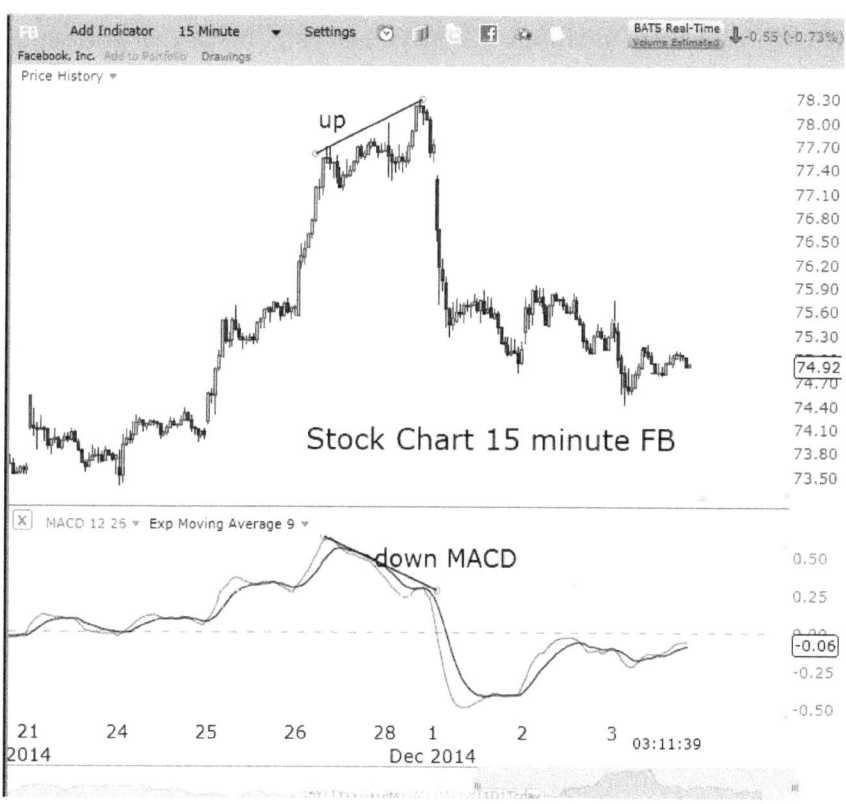

CANDLES

I don't place much emphasis on reading candlesticks but I do look for the doji and long wicks or tails. I think these patterns indicate a reversal in price action and usually do.

DOJI- a small candle representing indecision.

Long wicks and tails represent the unwillingness of price to go in that direction.

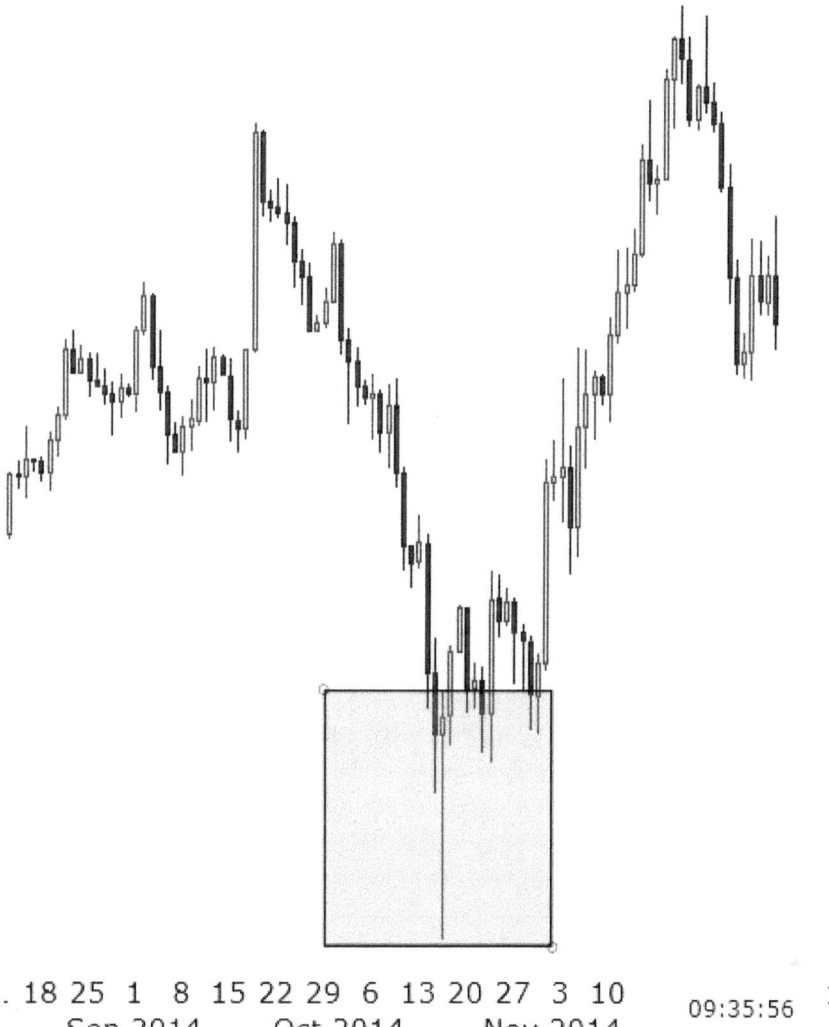

This long tail indicates that traders are not willing to take the price lower.

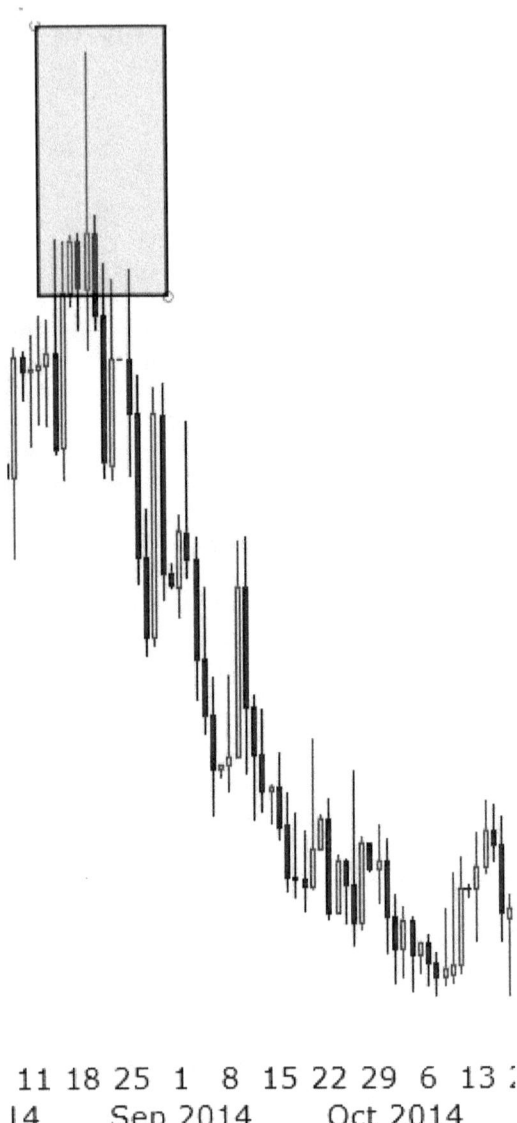

Price tends to run away from the indicated direction of the wick.

SUMMARY

These are the elements I use in my trading. Use them in conjunction with each other. Never rely on one pattern or indicator for your trading decision.

Trading is not easy but it does not have to be complicated. Keep it simple and develop your own system from the simple tasks that I have outlined in this book.

Order entry, money management and other important trading topics are explained in detail in my other publications.

Good luck and trade smart.

Dana DeCecco

Basic Charting Techniques

Dana DeCecco

www.ingramcontent.com/pod-product-compliance
Lightning Source LLC
Chambersburg PA
CBHW071825170526
45167CB00003B/1418